ART and
INVENTION

# Inventions
# in Music
## From the Monochord
## to MP3s

Lisa Hiton

Cavendish
Square

New York

Published in 2017 by Cavendish Square Publishing, LLC
243 5th Avenue, Suite 136, New York, NY 10016

Copyright © 2017 by Cavendish Square Publishing, LLC

First Edition

Website: cavendishsq.com

This publication represents the opinions and views of the author based on his or her personal experience, knowledge, and research. The information in this book serves as a general guide only. The author and publisher have used their best efforts in preparing this book and disclaim liability rising directly or indirectly from the use and application of this book.

CPSIA Compliance Information: Batch #CW17CSQ

All websites were available and accurate when this book was sent to press.

Library of Congress Cataloging-in-Publication Data

Names: Hiton, Lisa.
Title: Inventions in music : from the monochord to MP3s / Lisa Hiton.
Description: New York : Cavendish Square Publishing, [2017] |
Series: Art and invention | Includes bibliographical references and index.
Identifiers: LCCN 2016022433 (print) | LCCN 2016023624 (ebook) |
ISBN 9781502622976 (library bound) | ISBN 9781502622983 (E-book)
Subjects: LCSH: Musical inventions and patents. | Phonogram. |
Sound--Recording and reproducing--History.
Classification: LCC ML160 .H634 2017 (print) | LCC ML160 (ebook) |
DDC 784.192--dc23
LC record available at https://lccn.loc.gov/2016022433

Editorial Director: David McNamara
Editor: Caitlyn Miller
Copy Editor: Nathan Heidelberger
Associate Art Director: Amy Greenan
Designer: Joseph Macri
Production Assistant: Karol Szymczuk
Photo Research: J8 Media

Printed in the United States of America

# CONTENTS

Coded with instructions and a map, the song "Follow the Drinking Gourd" helped slaves escape from the South.

# INTRODUCTION:
# From Acoustic
# to Digital

We turn to the arts to understand the depths of human experience—from imagination, to anger, to beauty. It is through art that we are best able to empathize and transform ourselves and the world. The arts also help us define and understand cultures: music, dance, fashion, architecture, and drawing all signal nations and periods of time. And outside of our day-to-day lives, these forms play a prominent role in ritual. Religion, birth, life, graduation, death, marriage—they're all accompanied by different means of singing, chanting, dancing, and gathering together for a ceremony.

Music is a special practice that affects all individuals and communities. The origins of music come from our evolutionary capacities and developments in speech. While music was first a means for the species to survive, the urgency behind song continues to express the soul. In times before writing, music was an oral tradition, inherited by younger generations as a means of storytelling and mapping landscapes. Though this idea seems faraway, the mode of music as navigation has continued into times of social injustice. In America, slave owners did not educate their slaves in order to oppress them. Without being able to read and write in English, slaves experienced intellectual hardships to accompany the physical hardships of the lives they were forced into.

"Follow the Drinking Gourd" became a song of survival. Slaves using the Underground Railroad to escape enslavement would use this song's central figure, the Big Dipper (the "drinking gourd"), to navigate their way to freedom.

Our most contemporary memory of music as resistance to social injustice is perhaps counterculture. From rock 'n' roll to the early movements of soul, funk, and hip-hop, musicians and the communities they sang to joined in great masses to sing about peace and love during times of great war and turmoil.

From music's origin to now, many technologies have become intertwined with the medium. At first, this relationship came in the form of early instruments. Music, unlike visual art, is bound by time—the amount of time a given song, composition, or chant lasts as written by a composer. At the core of music is sound. It's no wonder that one of the earliest figures in music is Pythagoras from ancient Greece. He was the first person to understand music as part of nature—and as mathematically explainable. His philosophy and mathematic applications gave us more than geometry and ratios. It also gave us the **monochord**—a single-stringed instrument used to understand **pitch**. From this beginning, many other musical instruments came into the world: the lyre, the organ, flutes, guitars.

As different ways of singing and playing music developed over time, musicians often created new instruments to bring new sounds into the world. For example, Adolphe Sax invented the saxophone in the mid-1800s. Sax was a flutist and instrument maker. His work on single-reed instruments led him to create the saxophone, whose new sound became a central character in our image of jazz music. We often take for granted these ideas in music. We can't even imagine a time without the sound of a saxophone because it's so integral to our experience of listening to music.

Some of the most important inventions in music have been the ones that bring music to us. From early **analog** advances like transistor radios, phonographs, and **magnetic tape**, to our current digital technologies, like **MP3s**, DJ software, and Pro Tools, the role of the artist is more complex now.

During modern times, though, the artist and the inventor are often at odds. As the world advances and people have more access to music through radios, televisions, and the internet, the potential financial incentives and capacity for fame often drive commercial music. There's great power in the idea of a musician's work having worldwide impact. But behind the curtain, there are many people and institutions with their own agendas.

On the one hand, there's a sadness in this story. Artists still invent new sounds with their voices, new instruments, and new ways of making music. The middlemen in the industry, though, have taken so much power over the market that it's difficult for artists to have their own voice and succeed. Our mythic image of the artist can't seem to survive into the twenty-first century. While our image of music was once an ancient Greek at a harp, then a rockstar with a guitar, we now have the DJ at the center of commercial music. In this sense, our image of the artist has taken on new qualities and ideals. And yet, with new technologies, a remixing of the musician has offered a new image. The keys of a piano are now the keys of a computer. The audio engineer is no longer someone who sits behind a computer but rather a music star with an enigmatic instrument.

At the center of all of these changes is the art itself. To what extent our evolution changes the form matters less than the fact that our ability to make sound—to speak—has advanced into many technologies, many instruments, many languages. As culture changes, it's always artists whose ideas make us slow down and listen to what's truest in the world at a given moment in history.

Charles Darwin set off on a
voyage around the world in
1831, resulting in his theories of
evolution and natural selection.

# CHAPTER 1
# The Beginnings of Music

It's difficult to imagine a world before music. In fact, music is central to our understanding of the human condition. Our current understanding of music has so much to do with various technologies—the instruments and devices that allow us to listen to, share, perform, and produce music. But at the dawn of human civilization, the existence of music was much simpler. From the introduction of the human voice, to birdsongs, to monkeys drumming on hollow logs, music began as a basic impulse matched by organic materials.

In order to understand the beginning of music, we have to imagine silence. Then we add to it the first rhythms of nature, voice, and primitive instruments. The beginnings of music are made up of early musical instruments, early ideas about the origin (human impulse) behind music, and early depictions of music through other art forms.

# EARLY FIGURES

## Charles Darwin on Music and Evolution

One of the most sophisticated early explanations of the human voice as music comes from Charles Darwin. Darwin was the first thinker to present the world with the idea of evolution, and with it, natural selection. Though humans once believed man was an unchanging species, Darwin showed the biology behind evolution.

Darwin traveled the world for five years in the early 1830s. On his journey, he kept journals of his observations, where his studies of biology met with anthropology. Yet these observations were just that—only observations. The scientific method is not present in Darwin's journals. It would take a lot more empirical evidence to prove to the scientific community and to the public the merits about the idea. Darwin later shaped his observations into scientific theories. And like many theories, the theory of evolution radically changed our way of looking at the world. Darwin knew that his ideas would seem strange to people—even to many scientists. He waited over twenty years to publish his theories because of the consequences he knew he'd have to endure.

Darwin's radical theory of evolution is still considered controversial today as monotheism and science sometimes seem at odds with one another. The science is not contested, but the extent people *believe* what is presented by science is still a marker of one's politics or religious beliefs. Of the many ideas Darwin presented to prove the science behind evolution, the human voice as music was one of them. Darwin wrote:

> I cannot doubt that language owes its origin to the imitation and modification of various natural sounds, the voices of other animals, and man's own instinctive cries, aided by signs and gestures ... Some early progenitor of man probably first used his voice in producing true musical cadences, that is in singing, as do some of the gibbon-apes at the present day; and we may conclude from a widely-spread analogy, that this power would have

been especially exerted during the courtship of the sexes,—would have expressed various emotions, such as love, jealousy, triumph,—and would have served as a challenge to rivals. It is, therefore, probable that the imitation of musical cries by articulate sounds may have given rise to words expressive of various complex emotions.

Darwin suggests that the point of the human voice is directly related to sexual selection. Mating calls are a common practice in which creatures like birds and primates seek out mating partners. In some species, the use of voice is charming in a mating call. In other instances, a species may use voice aggressively to overpower other males to win the attention of the female. Today we know this theory about the origin of music as evolutionary musicology.

The human propensity for speech is, perhaps, the largest identifiable marker of our evolution into the twenty-first century—what other species seeks to read and write? Today, languages span multiple cultures and nations. These languages can be expressed in other forms, such as music, theater, poetry, film, dance, painting, and sculpture.

# EARLY TOOLS

How is it that we know about music of the early moments in human history? Nowadays, we have many resources to track our progress in all fields of study and society. We have books, libraries, oral traditions of storytelling, historians, anthropologists, and archaeologists preserving our collective knowledge in many different ways.

To understand times before knowledge was reliably tracked, we turn to some of our biggest resources about early music: archaeology and anthropology. By uncovering, preserving, and studying early objects, scholars have given us clues as to music's oldest roots.

# PREHISTORIC INSTRUMENTS

Prehistory means "before history." Prehistory encompasses all of history before the invention of written materials. Because there are no written documents to dig up, time is indicated to historians by geological markers. The three main eras of prehistory are the Stone Age, the Bronze Age, and the Iron Age. Unsurprisingly, the Stone Age begins with the first appearance of stone tools. This period began 2.5 million years ago. About 200,000 years ago, *Homo sapiens* came into the evolutionary cycle. From the outset, elaborate systems of burial are evident in the archaeological record from tools to build fires, play music, and early art. These multipart tools identify early *Homo sapiens*.

## The Human Voice

Some historians and scientists hypothesize that the human voice is the first instrument. Even before established patterns of language, the human voice was equipped to whistle, click, hum, cough, yawn, and sing. Archaeologists have found bones of the human throat that predate the oldest bone flutes from the Stone Age.

The hyoid bone is U-shaped and found in the neck. The oldest bone found to date is about sixty thousand years old. The hyoid bone allows for tongue support as well as greater movements of the tongue. This bone is common in many other mammals and fish, too.

It is important to note that the hyoid bone is not specific to male members of the species. While sexual selection may be part of the origin of music, **motherese**

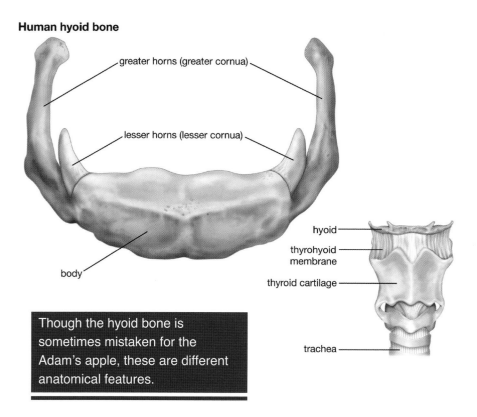

**Human hyoid bone**

greater horns (greater cornua)

lesser horns (lesser cornua)

hyoid

thyrohyoid membrane

body

thyroid cartilage

trachea

Though the hyoid bone is sometimes mistaken for the Adam's apple, these are different anatomical features.

is another matter for consideration. Motherese is the descriptor for vocal communications between infants and their mothers (of course, motherese extends to other caregivers as well). Today, we refer to this as "baby talk." It's common across many cultures and periods of time. Because infants aren't fully developed, voice is the intuitive first communication between parent and infant. This intuition could be genealogical. It could also relate to evolution—how a baby and mother can relate to each other in the infant's early stages as a means of safety. As we still practice in child raising today, these vocal cadences can match other kinds of anatomic music: footsteps, heartbeats, digestion, crying, etc. They are all signals for safety, nourishment, and survival. We even use these signals to communicate to the baby as it develops in utero. Today, listening to music before the baby is born is a common communication practice used by soon-to-be parents. Theoretically, the fetus is also shaped by learning the sounds and patterns of the internal body in which it grows, survives, and eventually outgrows. These primitive inheritances still hold in our development today.

## Early Percussion

Rhythm is likely an early marker of music. During the Stone Age, stones and bones were used as tools to help *Homo sapiens* survive. Fire building—a process completed by knocking stones together—is one example of early rhythm. Stone was also used to pound seeds, making it yet another early rhythm of the *Homo sapiens*. Hand clapping is another early model of patterned sound making. To this day, monkeys can be observed hitting hollow logs in aid of territory marking and protection.

Evolutionary biologists note that rhythm, beats, and tempo can be seen in *Homo sapiens* as they move from place to place. From the Stone Age through now, humans walk in patterned cadences as though time itself were an internal **metronome**.

## Bone Flutes

Of the many objects archaeologists have found, flutes are the first markers of musical instruments intended for music as we think of it today. Flutes were first made of bone. Bones can easily be hollowed (after marrow disintegrates or dries up). Once hollow, bones can be pierced with other sharp objects.

Some objects cannot be determined empirically as musical versus nonmusical. There are many examples of "phalangeal whistles," which archaeologists aren't sure were tools for music making, per se. Phalangeal whistles are finger bones pierced to function as the earliest version of the whistle. In 2008, archaeologists uncovered the oldest recognizable instrument to date: a vulture-bone flute. The forty-thousand-year-old artifact from the Stone Age was found in a cave in Germany. The flute was made from a griffon wing bone, which is naturally hollow. Carved into the flute are five holes. The end of the flute features a v-shaped cut out, which served as the mouthpiece. The flute maker would first have split the bone in half to evenly hollow it out. After fitting the halves back together, the flute maker would have used stone tools to make the mouthpiece and keys (holes).

As in Darwin's prediction, these first instruments were part of evolution. *Homo sapiens* were able to use these tools to communicate, out-surviving the now-extinct Neanderthal. The two most urgent primal impulses are reproduction and survival. The flute serves to show *Homo sapiens* were proficient in developing music for both.

Even though we use different materials to make flutes today, this basic design is kept most readily in what we now call a recorder. Recorders are often the earliest instruments given to young children in schools. They are small, affordable, and easy to learn. Xylophones are another common early instrument for similar reasons. As percussion and the flute were the first instruments based on the natural behavior of humans, such evolution is maintained today by these two early instruments.

# The Didgeridoo

This wind instrument provides an enigmatic sound from the past. Said to have first been made and used by Australian Aborigines about forty thousand years ago, the didgeridoo still exists today using more modern materials and building techniques. The oldest versions of the

Didgeridoos were originally used to accompany Australian Aborigines' dreamtime stories (or creation myths).

didgeridoo were made of eucalyptus wood after the flesh of the tree was devoured by termites. Some were also made of bamboo shoots. This instrument can be made in a variety of lengths. When played, the musician uses a technique of circular breathing—breathing in through the noise while simultaneously using the tongue and cheeks to play. Today, the didgeridoo is made of many modern materials (glass, clay, and leather, for example) and is still heard in contemporary music.

## The Bullroarer

A bullroarer is a simple instrument used in prehistoric and ancient times. Though historians and scientists have noted its presence in many places, its creation is most often credited to the Australian Aborigine culture. A bullroarer is a slat of wood with an attached cord. When spun around, it makes a vibrato sound that can be heard over long distances. Despite practical uses, this instrument was often used by Aborigines to ward off evil spirits and in other cultural rituals. It's one instrument that shows a leap from the evolutionary musicology view of music to a more Western realm of music as tied to culture, religion, emotion, and beliefs.

# ANCIENT INSTRUMENTS

As previously mentioned, evolutionary musicology considers the origins of music to be based on evolution, yet archaeologists have a more complex response to the origins of music. Music, by definition as we call it today, involves an emotional and even spiritual response. As *Homo sapiens* evolved in ancient times, instruments and writing create an effect of musical harmony and wholeness as the desired effect. The effects led to the incorporation of music into spiritual rites.

# The Shofar Horn

The shofar is a ram horn, used by Jews during various religious practices. The horn can make a variety of sounds, similar to a didgeridoo. A shofar is most commonly used today during Rosh Hashanah (the Jewish New Year) and Yom Kippur (the Day of Atonement). During Rosh Hashanah, the portion of the Torah that tells the story of Abraham bringing his son Isaac as a sacrifice to God is read. Just as Abraham is about to make the sacrifice, he sees a ram that he sacrifices instead. The shofar blasts represent many mythic symbols related to repentance during this time of year.

# MUSIC and MUSICIANS of the NEAR EAST

There are still wide gaps in our knowledge of early human history. Yet evidence exists from early world cultures. Some of the first markers of human understanding of music come from the Sumerians.

Sumer was the first urban civilization that existed in Mesopotamia during ancient times. Sumerians used **cuneiform** script to write in their language. Cuneiform is considered proto-writing, or writing with symbols. "Cuneiform" means "wedge-shaped." Sumerians inscribed their language into clay tablets with sharp reeds in these wedge-shaped pictograms and logographs.

Sumerian tablets from the fourteenth century BCE have been found with ancient cuneiform markings. Today, scholars have interpreted the markings as the oldest known piece of music ever discovered. Dr. Anne Draffkorn Kilmer has interpreted the cuneiform into musical notation as we can read it today. You can even hear versions of the world's oldest song on the internet!

# SONGLINES

Though many historians and scientists disagree about the origins of music, or how to define music, there is one strange primitive development within sound that suggests an inherent impulse toward song: **songlines**.

During prehistoric times, humans began using song as a means of mapping. There were not yet means of writing down path markers. Indigenous peoples of Australia (among others) used oral mythology as a means of navigating and remembering the land they'd explored. In Aboriginal tribes, those who'd gone out and explored the land would retell the story for the benefit of the tribe. The path is marked by sung lyrics. When another member of the tribe went out to walk the same path, if the song was repeated, it was easy to retrace the same path taken by the first person. This guided walking through song and dance brought other tribe members to the same landmarks that the original person had seen. Some paths are evident by depressions in the ground. This can be seen in Australia and other places where songlines were used as early forms of creation myth.

This practice suits both the predictions of evolutionary musicology and our current understanding of the arts as related to the beauty and resilience of the human spirit. Aborigines can walk hundreds of miles of desert, noting details along the way, and easily navigate through without error by using songlines. Along many of these paths, there are accompanying glyphs to punctuate the landmarks needed to get through the path.

Fewer songlines survive now because of colonial developments in the nineteenth and twentieth centuries, which displaced and continue to displace many communities.

A man plays the shofar horn to mark the opening of a synagogue in Israel.

Our Western culture credits Pythagoras and his monochord with the birth of music as we know it today. However, these tablets prove that there were other civilizations invested in music, music theory, and music writing even earlier than the ancient Greeks. Likewise, the oldest tablet found so far seems to be a cult hymn. As Sumerians made up a robust urban civilization, Hebrew and Arabic cultures burgeoned in other nearby cities. As with cultures today, it's safe to guess that they all learned ideas from each other, which led to further development.

Along with these ancient tablets, artifacts of Sumerian musicians have been found. Pictograms on the tablets show singers, musicians, instruments, dancing, and rituals involving music. Dr. Kilmer has studied many of the instruments that were found near these ancient tablets. An eleven-stringed bovine lyre is an important instrument of the Sumerian past. Dug up from Sumerian graves, the lyre and wind instruments suggest that music was a central part of life and culture during ancient times—and not just for the Greeks. Human evolution works across nations as illuminated by the very existence of these artifacts, which predate Pythagoras and his monochord.

After years of studying Sumerian ruins, Dr. Kilmer and her colleagues have been able to rebuild and replicate these ancient instruments. Further, with diligent study, they've been able to translate parts of the cuneiform tablets, which suggest the appropriate means of tuning and playing these early instruments.

By replicating and playing these instruments and the texts that went with them to the best of our ability, we can be closer to the musicians of the ancient Near East. By following the script of our ancient forefathers, it's clear that Sumerians were beginning to understand **harmony** and its other parts. The bovine lyre, especially, represents these musical ideas in the culture. Because there were so many strings in perfect **intervals**, tuning and playing them according to the cuneiform script indicates that multiple strings were played at once, as in **chords** and harmonies. Scales, pitch, and **octaves** and other intervals were all present in these early artifacts. From then on, much of musical practice has stayed the same, especially in Western music. We still tune our instruments, practice scales, and use mathematic intervals to achieve that mythic atmosphere called harmony.

# MUSIC from PREHISTORY to ANCIENT HISTORY

The key change in music development from prehistory to ancient history is the turn from survival to style. Because of the evolutionary advancement of speech (the effect of which is higher thinking), sound and story become a prevailing marker of the species. Beyond survival, style stands to give us music in the Western sense we still know it by today. The introduction of style—or mathematically perfected sound—resulted in new language about music including harmony, chords, octaves, pitch, and melody. And these words are the cause of new thoughts and new emotions. One couldn't express feelings of or beliefs in harmony before these art instruments entered human life and consciousness. It is this seed of music—the one that includes emotional intelligence and imaginative flexibility—from which our musical culture still grows.

Filippo Bonanni's engraving of the monochord dates to 1723, demonstrating the instrument's continued importance centuries after its invention.

Monocordo

# CHAPTER 2
# The Monochord

P laying music is still, to this day, influenced by the monochord, an ancient Greek instrument made to understand musical pitch. Pythagoras's invention consists of one simple vibrating string. Pythagoras is a name we mostly associate with math. But Pythagoras applied math to many facets of life. In the case of sound, Pythagoras was determined to understand why certain sounds, when overlaid and played in particular orders, sounded better than other combinations. This line of questioning has roots in philosophy and spirituality: What does "better" even mean? For Pythagoras, pursuing such questions through objective reasoning became his obsession.

## The INVENTION ITSELF
### Pythagoras's Obsession with Harmony

As the myth tells it, Pythagoras first conceived of the monochord when walking past a brazier's shop. Ripe with thoughts and questions about sound in his mind, he noticed the sound of metal—workmen pounding metal on an anvil. Pythagoras paused to listen and intellectualize the different pitches he heard. He went into the brass shop and studied the tools.

Pythagoras's invention forever changed music.

In his own home, he replicated the tools he'd seen. He made an arm of wood extending out from the wall. He attached four strings to the end of the arm, hanging in regular intervals from one another. He lay the strings tautly across the wood to the arm's other end. At the end of each string, he placed a weight: 12 pounds (5.4 kilograms), then 9 pounds (4 kg), then 8 pounds (3.6 kg), then 6 pounds (2.7 kg). As he played—or caused the vibration of— each string, he listened for "better" sounds, which were considered celestial phenomena at the time. When the first and fourth strings were played together, something magical happened: Pythagoras heard harmony. Today, we know this interval as an octave. Because the tension of the first string was double that of the fourth, the 2:1 ratio caused an octave to be heard at once. It's no surprise that the figure whose greatest contributions to math and the world are related to ratios was the first to understand the mechanics of harmony.

From playing with strings, Pythagoras ended up understanding that changing the length of the string would change its frequency when plucked. He devised a monochord. He stretched a single string across a sound box. He fixed the string at both ends. Finally, he crafted a bridge that could be moved so that the string could express various pitches. Imagine a guitar missing five of its strings and your finger as a moveable bridge. If you place your finger at various points of the string and pluck it, you'll hear different pitches.

The monochord proved the mathematical properties of pitch. When the string vibrates without the bridge placed anywhere, one pitch occurs. When the bridge is placed to effectively halve the string, a pitch an octave higher will be heard. This 2:1 ratio is the underpinning of the octave. It also gave Pythagoras's followers proof of beauty and harmony as having mathematical explanations.

# PYTHAGORAS of SAMOS
## (CA. 570—CA. 495 BCE)

Pythagoras was an early pioneer in math and physics. In ancient times, fields of study and thinking were broad and few. His ability to apply math to physical phenomena made him the father of geometry, ratios, and early physics. His most famous doctrine is "Things are numbers." According to physicist Demetris Nicolaides, Pythagoras proved that "the phenomena of nature are describable by equations and numbers." Our understanding of music as being mathematical in nature comes from these ideas in ancient Greece.

Pythagoras is a figure of liberal arts in the oldest sense of the tradition. His ways of thinking crossed over into every part of life. Whether he had an idea about sound or numbers, his methods of thinking—known now as philosophy—were the earliest forms of the scientific method. He'd make observations in the world, then figure out a hypothesis to test. This is seen in the myth about the monochord. Though some parts of the myth likely aren't true, the story represents the early ways of Western thinking across many disciplines, including philosophy, science, math, and the arts.

## Harmony and Its Other Parts

As Pythagoras used his new, simple instrument to understand harmony, he was able to articulate the details he observed. The 2:1 ratio wasn't the only ratio that mattered to making something that sounded beautiful. A pair weighing 3:2 (in music, a fifth apart) also sounded beautiful. Pythagoras began building other basic instruments to test these simple ratios. No matter what he used—hammers, bells, pipes, cups with water—the results were the same. When he kept the ratios simple, the sounds were pleasant. He noticed this also stayed true regardless of the way the sound was made—by pluck, blow, or strike.

Within these sound ratios, a whole language about harmony came to fruition. As Pythagoras plucked the strings of his first machine, he realized the different length or tension of the chord resulted in different sounds. Similar to pressing a finger down on a guitar string, these single sounds produce different pitches. We now refer to these sounds with defined pitch as musical **notes**.

The blending of notes make more complex, definite sounds thanks to ratios. After the octave and the fifth, 4:3 is the fourth, and 5:4 is the third.

We often take for granted what we hear. All day, we hear noises: cars on the streets, people talking, sirens as a truck passes by, the whir of a laundry machine, crickets in the summer grass. All of these can be perceived as either noise (unwanted sound) or music, in which the brain can arrange these sounds into a pleasant arrangement of the world. The ear is perhaps the most mysterious instrument of all. It reads vibrations and processes them, translating them into music or noise, playing on our moods and emotions.

Within the discovery of harmony, a whole way of discussing intentioned sound—music—came into the public consciousness. Two of the most important parts of music as we know it today are the scale and the octave. A scale is a set of notes occurring in evenly spaced progression from which melodies can be written. The most common scale we know is the **diatonic scale**—claimed by Pythagoras himself. These seven notes go from A to G and make up most of Western music today.

From the scale comes the octave. It wouldn't be enough to have only seven notes to express all of the things that an artist wants to express in music. So, when we get to the end of the seven notes, we can keep adding more. The next note, the eighth, is given the same letter name as the starting note of the scale, and it starts the same scale all over again, in a higher octave. An octave represents the interval between these two notes, the first and the eighth. The upper note is twice the frequency of the lower note (here comes math again!). You could think of this like markings on a ruler. The long line that marks the end of one inch also marks the beginning of the next one.

From the octave, we get the key of a song. Whichever note starts the scale that is used in the song becomes the song's key. So if the first note of the scale is A, then the song is in the key of A. This relates to an actual key on a given instrument—a piano key, for example—as well as the poetic idea behind the song: to unlock the door of the song and play the notes given to you begins with the key.

We can see this whole system represented in singing by the solfège system. Many of us might know of this from the musical *The Sound of Music*, in which the Von Trapp family learns the song "Do-Re-Mi." We can represent notes on a scale by this system: do, re, mi, fa, sol, la, ti, do. This system of learning music didn't enter the world until the Middle Ages, well after Pythagoras's time. In this system, every tone has a name in relation to other tones. The tones can be replaced by words, humming, or other sounds when making a song. But this system is used to learn how to sing and how to sight-read music as it's written today.

Another of Pythagoras's discoveries when experimenting with sound relates to the quality of sounding pleasant. But how do we get to harmony—to that *pleasant* sound? When notes are played at the same time, they may sound good to the ear. This combination is consonant. If notes played together sound harsh or tense, these sounds are considered dissonant. The sounds played together are

# LISSAJOUS FIGURES

Lissajous figures are still used throughout physics. They are even simulated digitally these days.

By the mid-nineteenth century, **tuning forks** were a more popular way to tune an instrument than the monochord. French mathematician Jules Lissajous designed an experiment by placing a mirror on top of a tuning fork and casting light at it as it made a pitch. He also placed another tuning fork at a right angle to the first. When the light and sound travelled, beautiful shapes fell onto the wall or black paper placed behind the experiment. These visualizations of sound (now called Lissajous figures) show its mathematic patterns and perfections. Harmony can be translated into many forms.

known as chords. Next time you're at a piano, try to play two or three keys at once. Do they make a pleasant sound? Or a discordant sound? If they sound pleasant, it's likely that you've just played a standard chord used in music practices today. Pythagoras discovered that the simpler the ratio was between the frequencies of two notes—for example the 2:1 of the octave or the 3:2 of the fifth—the more consonant the notes would sound when played together. Conversely, more complicated ratios—like 6:13 or 11:15—would yield more dissonant intervals.

# RECEPTION

## Music as We Know It

Pythagoras was beloved by many, especially his students. He was known for great teachings in philosophy, religion, science, math, and of course, music. But he was also known for teaching a way of life. The students at his school in Croton, Italy, had a shared canon of texts from school, but they also bonded through their shared lifestyle. The school was open to men and women. Pythagoras modeled an ascetic way of life for all—a life that included exercise, vows of silence, and vegetarianism. He also helped students bond by instilling the value of privacy from outsiders. This took form in the secrecy afforded the discoveries made by himself, his colleagues, and his students. It is this kind of elitism that is still perpetuated in our university system and in many industries.

This way of life was focused on the value of learning in and of itself. There was no goal for students to end up with fancy business degrees, signing bonuses, and other fiscally motivated outcomes. Rather, the cause and effect of education was to become a learned and cultured person in the community and the world at large.

To value all the subjects equally allows them to be of equal value. It also supported conversations between and within these areas of study. Nowadays, we leave thinking to philosophy, performance to music, and the scientific method to scientific experiments. If Pythagoras hadn't used all of those practices together, the world would not have had the monochord or our whole system of regulating musical notes for the sake of performance.

# A Change in Beliefs

Before Pythagoras, people thought that human law was at the forefront of existence. By discovering harmony in nature, Pythagoras's findings changed our understanding of human existence. Pythagoras went on to show that the universe was organized according to musical ratio— eventually leading to the Pythagorean Theorem. In those ancient times, number theory and music theory were equally mystic to people. And as such, people believed music could be played to conjure and change the ethos of its listeners. If the appropriate music was played, the species could process complex emotions as a community.

For Pythagoras, this discovery was beyond song making. He believed these experiments showed that there is harmony in all of nature, and this harmony stems from mathematics. Just as cosmologists would prove that Earth is round and that the sun is the center of the universe, Pythagoras's discovery *that numbers can describe occurrences* shook the prevailing beliefs of his time. Pythagoras realized that if ratios could describe sound, then they could also describe other enigmatic phenomena: lightness, wetness, weather, the movement of heavenly bodies (planets), and everything else imaginable and tangible. This was a radical new design for the universe.

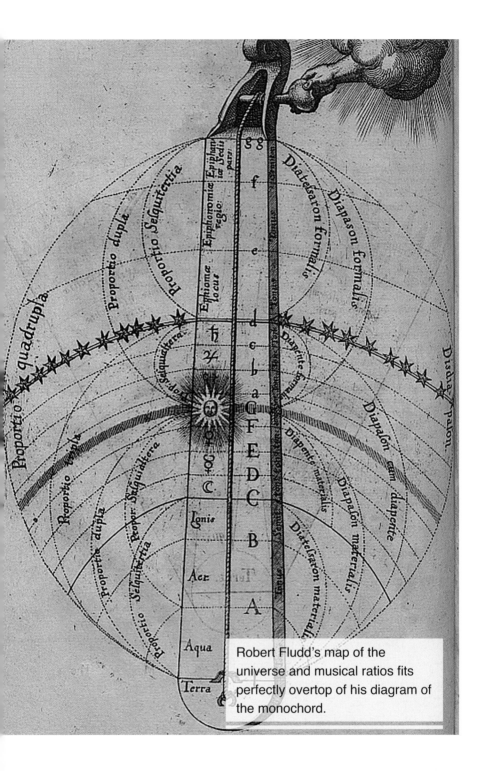

Robert Fludd's map of the universe and musical ratios fits perfectly overtop of his diagram of the monochord.

# LEGACIES

## The Monochord's Revival

In 1618, cosmologist Robert Fludd devised a new monochord, the divine monochord. Back then, physics and the occult were not such disparate studies. Both were interested in heavenly bodies, which we call planets today. Calling them heavenly bodies shows the relationship to the sky and religion that was believed at the time. Fludd published a work called *Mundante Monochord* to describe the relationship between the scientific and occult qualities of sound. Fludd describes tuning the monochord string as sounding the harmonic ratios of the universe.

Fludd's monochord diagram shows the musical scale as a model of the universe. Diagraming music became a popular way of showing the math and science behind the art form. Artists and scientists alike were able to be in dialogue about this mysterious form of expression because of these new ways of understanding sound.

## INVENTIONS and DISCOVERIES CAUSED by the MONOCHORD

The lyre, a lap harp, was a prominent instrument in ancient Greece. Known as a commoners' instrument, we might compare it to the ukulele of today. Like a guitar, the lyre was played by strumming, often with a pick. The monochord allowed the tuning of this instrument to be regulated. It also presented means by which songs could be learned and made, offering new language to the sound that resulted from playing the instrument.

Eventually, the monochord led to a lyre-specific tuning device. A kollops was made out of leather, a wooden peg, and a crossbar. The device was used to adjust the tuning for many stringed instruments such as the lyre and the harp.

After the lyre and the kollops came the harmonograph. Similar to the first, mythic, rendering of Pythagoras's experiment, the harmonograph was built to hold multiple taut cords with various weights on the end. The harmonograph involves a drawing implement placed at the end of these weights to visually represent the relationships between various pitches. The harmonograph can be built to host lateral movements or rotary movements.

In a lateral harmonograph, a table holds two cords with weight on the end. The weights swing laterally, like a pendulum. The two pendulums swing in a perpendicular fashion. When the cords are manipulated, various results will show the relationship between harmonic ratios.

The rotary harmonograph can host three cords. The pendulums swing in circular fashions. When combining the three resulting markings, more complex shapes can represent harmonies and chords.

# A ROSE by ANY OTHER NAME …

The monochord became a cross-cultural instrument. Single-stringed instruments have many stories from many different parts of history. Sometimes, they are tuning devices, and other times they are used for music making. Pythagoras holds the patent over the myth, of course.

The berimbau is a single-stringed percussion instrument in Brazilian and Portuguese cultures. The diddley bow is a single-stringed American instrument, highly associated with the blues sound. An ektara is a single-stringed instrument very similar to the monochord, used in Egypt, India, Pakistan, and Bangladesh. It's even said that Pythagoras may have used this as inspiration for his monochord during his travels around Mesopotamia.

In a way, our understanding of music itself hasn't changed so much from ancient times. While we will see many industries interfere with music and musicians, the true artists maintain a sense of mysticism about the art form. At their core, music and speech are about expression of higher-order thinking and feeling. Many people learn to sing at their religious institutions. Pythagoras was known to have been the first philosopher—a lover of wisdom. Music and numbers collided to show intervals, ratios, and progression to Pythagoras and his disciples. Throughout many periods of music, these basic ideas are remembered and reinterpreted through new ideas, sounds, and instruments. Music is still our means of bonding, emotional expression, cosmic curiosity, and survival.

# T. A. EDISON.
## Phonograph.

**No. 227,679.**  **Patented May 18, 1880.**

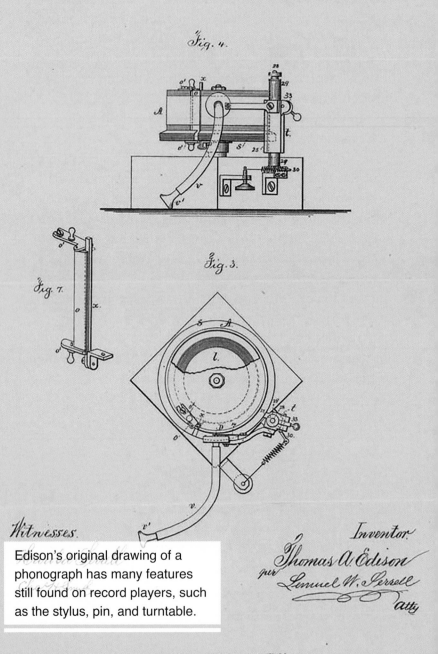

Edison's original drawing of a phonograph has many features still found on record players, such as the stylus, pin, and turntable.

Witnesses.

Inventor:
Thomas A. Edison
per Lemuel W. Serrell
atty

# CHAPTER 3
# The Phonograph

Today, as record players are making a comeback as retro novelties, it's important to note that their beginning marked a huge change in music. The first record player, the phonograph, was invented in 1877 by Thomas Edison. Phonographs were the first machines that could both record and reproduce sound. Prior to the phonograph, simple machines could reproduce sound. But the same machine could not yet capture and play back auditory information. The ability to perform both of those tasks makes the phonograph one of the most significant contributions to music and to our communication abilities from the late nineteenth century until now.

## INVENTIONS That LED to the PHONOGRAPH

### Phonautograph

Édouard-Léon Scott was a printer by trade at a time when typesetting still required a love of manual labor and rigor. Scott's 1857 **phonautograph** transcribed sound waves into undulating lines in real time. In order to make this machine, Scott modeled it off of the human ear. He designed a machine to function in parallel to the ear by using a small funnel-like object as the ear and ear canal. He then placed parchment over the small end of the funnel. To that he attached bristles. When sound was played into the opening of the machine, the parchment and bristles would vibrate (with different frequencies based on the pitches played) and trace a line onto a moving, lampblack-coated paper (an earlier version of carbon paper). The resulting paper of drawn waveforms was known as the **phonautogram**. It wouldn't be for another two decades that people would begin to realize the information contained in a phonautogram would be sufficient to replicate the sounds that had been recorded.

# Paleophone

French poet and aspiring scientist Charles Cros deposited a sealed envelope full of ideas for photoengraving to the French Academy of Sciences in April of 1877. This standard procedure—still used today by writers, artists, and innovators—was a means to protect the originality of his ideas in case someone else tried to steal them later. Similar to Scott of the phonautograph, the world of printing was Cros's entry into making recordings of music. Metal printing plates had entered into the world of publishing. Cros figured there must be a way to not only record sound, but to use the resulting document to also play the sound back, as in line drawings transferred to a metal plate, used to print and reprint a given image or piece of text.

His letter described a **paleophone**. The word comes from the Greek for "ancient sound." More poetically for this French poet, though, the French *voix du passé* means "voice of the past." This machine combined the phonautogram with the idea of photoengraving so that a **diaphragm** with an attached **stylus** could ride along a groove—a groove of the initial recorded sound—and thus, play back the sound or music that was just recorded. Cros described both a flat metal surface and a metal cylinder being spun at the same speed as the original recording in order to replicate the sound with precision.

Today, we have timing written at the beginning of sheet music in the form of indications of tempo, or beats per minute (often organized into groupings of 4/4 time, 3/4 time, etc.), and we also have standardized speeds as settings on a record player. Even for those of us who don't use a record player, anything mixed by a DJ or made digitally uses these rules and notations to fix the speed of a song. Similarly, the metronome's various settings can help us play music at different, consistent speeds.

# The INVENTION ITSELF

While other inventors thus far had ties to inventing sound recording devices through their own artistic practices—from music, to writing, to printing, and more—Thomas Edison's desire to invent a machine that could record and reproduce sound began with the telegraph. He envisioned a machine that could receive a telegraph signal and then speak the message aloud. But while he was trying to improve the telegraph transmitter, he noticed something peculiar. The paper tape moving through the machine made noise resembling a human voice. When rolling the paper through at higher speeds, the voice became more decipherable.

## The Mechanics of the Phonograph

In his own accounts of inventing the phonograph, Edison claims that he was ripe for the discovery because of his previous work with the telephone:

Scott's phonautograph was the earliest
known sound recording device. The
tuning fork's vibrations were recorded
onto blackened paper.

I knew of how to work a pawl connected to the diaphragm; and this engaging a ratchet-wheel served to give continuous rotation to a pulley. This pulley was connected by a cord to a little paper toy representing a man sawing wood. Hence, if one shouted: "Mary had a little lamb," etc., the paper man would start sawing wood. I reached the conclusion that if I could record the movements of the diaphragm properly, I could cause such records to reproduce the original movements imparted to the diaphragm by the voice, and thus succeed in recording and reproducing the human voice.

As in Cros's ideas for a stylus attached to a diaphragm, Edison used a grooved cylinder as the basis for his experiment. He then covered it in tinfoil. As we know still, tinfoil is an easy surface to tamper with. It folds and dents without much effort at all. The stylus very swiftly recorded the movements of the diaphragm onto the tinfoil.

In 1877, Edison set up his machine. As he cranked the cylinder around and spoke "Mary Had a Little Lamb" into the open end of a cone, the machine's stylus recorded the sound. And when he cranked the machine around the newly drawn line again, the machine talked back in perfect reproduction.

# The Mechanics of Recording

Edison, initially, was stubbornly bound to his recording cylinders. While his original drafts do show that a disc was a possible alternative, the grooved can resulted in a consistent, reliable velocity. Though it was more scientifically correct, issues of storage and multiple prints quickly became a problem.

Cros's thought-experiment was tested by Edison and other innovators in the great race to invention. They could

Thomas Edison beside his invention

not figure out a way to record on a disc that was easy to replicate for multiple copies, among other things. Cros died in 1888 at the age of forty-five. He never got to reap the benefits of his idea. And just before Cros's death, Emile Berliner came along to disrupt the industry of both playing and recording music with two new inventions: the gramophone record and the gramophone.

# RECEPTION

## Phonograph Parlors

Like many early machines, phonographs weren't cheap. Eventually, phonograph parlors became popular in major American cities. Unlike the lightbulb or the telephone, the ability to record oneself or to listen to a machine speak was a luxury, not a necessity. Customers could pay to record a disc or cylinder of themselves speaking. At the time, this was very radical. No one had ever before heard their own voice played back to them. There were not, for example, answering machines on phones. And music hadn't yet become a full-blown industry. People had never been able to listen to their own voice separate from speaking, and many found the experience of hearing their recordings to be very haunting. It was the first moment in time where the idea that a person's voice could come from beyond the grave came into being.

Another listening experience came in the form of an early jukebox. The phonograph was rigged so that it wouldn't start until a coin was inserted. Eventually, this led to a basic recording studio setup. Artists could mass-produce their work by recording on these "master" phonographs. And as the recording technologies advanced, the process became easier and easier.

# The GRAMOPHONE RECORD and the GRAMOPHONE

Unlike the cylinder of Edison, Emile Berliner's disc recorded sound in a horizontal fashion. As described by Cros, Berliner's gramophone used a lampblack disc. The disc would rotate at a consistent speed while a stylus moved across it. By putting a wax or varnish on the opaque lampblack disc, the stylus line created a photoengraving, as imagined by Cros. Berliner then dipped the disc into chromatic acid, essentially locking a groove into the disc where the stylus had scraped the wax coating away. These discs were also known as phonograph records. With some modifications in technology over time, we simply refer to them as "vinyl" or "records" today.

On the brink of invention, Berliner started the US Berliner Gramophone Company. As the phonograph and the gramophone discs continued to be modified, a major issue for users was hand-cranking the turntable. It was very difficult to ensure that the motion of the disc or cylinder would be steady. Berliner's company sought engineering advice for a wind-up spring motor. In the end, the difference between a gramophone and a phonograph was the ability to record sound. While the phonograph did both, the gramophone simply played records. Though we don't use the term today, the object and its historic significance can be seen at the Grammys. The award is the shape of a gramophone, and the name still recalls this early instrument, which changed the mass availability of music for all.

# LEGACIES

## Thomas Edison, the Wizard of Menlo Park

Edison invented many objects we still use today. But it wasn't until he invented the phonograph that he became known as "The Wizard of Menlo Park." Menlo Park was the name of the city in New Jersey where he worked on most of his experiments. Edison, after many scientific failures and going broke, eventually worked for telegraph engineers. After working on projects to improve the telephone, Edison's innovations were bought out.

Edison took his new fortune and went to New Jersey. He ended up with two pieces of land in the Menlo Park neighborhood. One building served as a home for his family and another as a laboratory. It was the world's first research and development center. The phonograph was his first successful invention at Menlo Park Laboratory, just one year after the lab opened. Within a year of inventing the phonograph, the machine was known around the world.

People came from all over to see "The Wizard of Menlo Park" and the facility that spurred invention. Edison commissioned builders to expand on his laboratory to host a machine shop, library, and office within the complex. He called this the "Invention Factory." Edison's sudden fame did not slow his brilliance. By 1879, he would figure out his next big invention: an incandescent lightbulb.

## The Recording Industry

Around the same time that Berliner was working on the gramophone, Alexander Graham Bell—most known for his invention of the telephone—decided to improve the phonograph. The phonograph was a feat of genius, yes, but it also didn't work that well yet. It was difficult to hear the recordings. The tinfoil used to make the recordings tore easily. The stylus was too finicky and difficult to adjust. Sound was often distorted and only worsened with more playbacks. Bell's Volta Laboratory (his own version of a Menlo Park) finally got the patents needed to improve the machine and to record into wax.

To Edison's shock and awe, his phonograph worked on the first try. And although fame and fortune immediately followed, Edison was already deep into his efforts with the lightbulb and developing electric light and power systems to also improve the phonograph. It's no surprise that after building the telephone, Bell would be ripe to work on the phonograph improvements that Edison could not. Bell had a deep understanding of how sound travels and of the power these widespread inventions could have in the lives of the public. For Bell and his associates at his Volta Laboratory, more work would be required than Edison's one-time build for a phonograph. After many experiments, a new machine resulted: the **graphophone** (an improved version of the phonograph, not be confused with the gramophone).

Bell worked with his cousin, Chichester Bell, to improve the phonograph's means of recording to make the graphophone. Chichester Bell was a professor of chemistry. He suggested using a process that would serve as a photograph of the sound:

> A jet of bichromate of potash solution, vibrated by the voice, was directed against a glass plate immediately in front of a slit, on which light was concentrated by means of a lens. The jet was so

Bell's Dictaphone was used primarily by businessmen for taking notes and recording meetings.

arranged that the light on its way to the slit had to pass through the nappe and as the thickness of this was constantly changing, the illumination of the slit was also varied. By means of a lens … an image of this slit was thrown upon a rotating gelatine-bromide plate, on which accordingly a record of the voice vibrations was obtained.

These ideas went beyond the testing of a simple machine. The Bell men and Charles Sumner Tainter set out to design an experimental apparatus. It required a lot of searching for materials all over different American cities in order to build the new machine. The experimental machines they made included disc and cylinder tapes. They were somewhat successful at recording in a new way, using wax over the grooves on their discs and cylinders. But it would be Berliner's gramophone record that would serve as a jump-start to music as more than performance, but instead, as an industry.

## Beyond Music

The endeavor of the phonograph and graphophone was outside of the music world. Both Edison and Bell were trying to invent a device that recorded speaking. It wasn't foremost for music, but rather for businessmen and conducting meetings. An invention that *both* recorded sound and played it back sought to change, in their minds, the day-to-day lives of ordinary men—and the women who were their secretaries. Like many inventions, the crossover into music invented a whole new industry.

The graphophone and gramophone represent a split in the use of sound recording and playback in the world. The graphophone went on, as the men intended, to address business needs. After founding the

Volta Graphophone Company, Bell kept working on experimental machines. Eventually, he created a sister company, Dictaphone, which produced dictation machines.

By 1907, the Volta Graphophone Company merged with the American Graphophone Company to create Columbia Records. They trademarked the name "Dictaphone" and continued using wax cylinders for vertical voice recordings. This technology lasted through World War II. The two world wars were the first fought with this technology, a technology that utterly changed the West's relationship to communications and intelligence. After Word War II, a new machine brought to the world by the makers of Dictaphone came into being: the Dictabelt.

Instead of a wax cylinder, a plastic belt was used for recording. Not only did dictation machines change business, journalism, and war, but they became the means of recording goings-on in court.

Meanwhile, the gramophone and Berliner's invention of horizontal recording pervaded the ability to hear and share music. Time and time again, Berliner's approach to playback impacted music and history. His gramophone record is the pioneer model for analog sound storage, which lived on from initial acoustic recordings into electric recording. It is his gramophone record that invited large changes in the music industry: advancement in **microphones**, the invention of **headphones**, portable music machines, adjustments to the turntable, reinventing the stylus, and beyond.

In the 1920s, advancements in radio in conjunction with the Great Depression led to huge financial despair in the business of record sales. From this economic-historic crisis, audio **fidelity** and commercialization of music advanced. The larger record companies were able to survive until the revival of sales in the 1930s. Transportable radios served as a threat, but with more money to spend, record companies were able to, for example, print vinyl discs for soldiers during World War II. These discs were difficult to break. By the end of the war, home vinyl became more popular. As with the graphophone, the impact of war on the content of music and the industry was tremendous. Sound technologies across the board changed the way people were able to understand the world—from culture, to politics, to journalism, and beyond.

It would be with the invention of magnetic tape that technological development would again change the world of music and the world at large.

MONITOR 2

4-TRACK STEREO DECK

PAUSE    REC

MIC ─●─ LINE

REC

VU                 VU

REC MODE
STEREO
LEFT    RIGHT

TAPE
SELECTOR
LOW NOISE

WIDE RANGE

These clunky reels of tape mark the first turning point in the evolution from analog recording to digital recording.

# CHAPTER 4
# The Magnetic Tape

I t seems a long way to go from early instruments and early recording devices (like the phonograph) all the way to our digital world of music. Fritz Pfleumer's invention of the magnetic tape is a critical bridge between these developments. Like many of the world's great thinkers and inventors, Pfleumer changed music and communication profoundly with his invention. Not only did the magnetic tape revolutionize the music industry, it also forever altered the relationship between the general public and transmissions of the human voice: political, journalistic, personal, and musical transmissions were all affected. And, like many great ideas, the mythology around the invention of magnetic tape is wild compared to our expectations of the scientific method.

## INVENTIONS That LED to MAGNETIC TAPE

### "Some Possible Forms of Phonograph"

The idea of magnetic recording was first thought of and documented by Oberlin Smith. Smith was an American engineer. Born in Ohio, he ended up starting a machine shop in New Jersey the same year that Edison invented the phonograph at his Menlo Park Laboratory. In 1888, Smith wrote a short piece for *Electrical World*, a British journal, that described recording sound through the use of magnetic impressions. He'd been dabbling in magnetic recording on cotton and silk threads, which he'd woven with steel dust, wire clippings, and a variety of other combinations. He wasn't able to make a working machine, so he thought he'd present his ideas to the world.

In Smith's brief thought-experiment, he described a few methods of magnetic recording alongside two diagrams of how the recording would work. His primary suggestion was to use a thread in which steel dust or wire clippings could be suspended. The diagram showed a basic reel as part of a phonograph. The thread began at the mouthpiece or microphone. The microphone with diaphragm would still have the spring and indenting needle (stylus) of Edison's phonograph. He showed a reel for his magnetizable thread to pass through to generate heat and a smaller reel where the thread is collected for later playback. He thought the currents between the microphone and the thread would allow for a more advanced recording and playback experience for users. The sound would be amplified, consistent, and less distorted in quality.

Smith also offered a description of a similar process that used a hard steel wire. He claimed in the article that it would be a less plausible approach because of several factors, including cost. None of these diagrams manifested into a model for experimentation during Smith's life. But these ideas were the seeds of Valdemar Poulsen's 1899 magnetic wire recorder.

Poulsen's ingenuity in using an alternating current to make a magnetic recording benefits us every day that we use electricity.

# The Telegraphone

Valdemar Poulsen was born in 1869. Before age thirty, this Danish engineer created the world's first magnetic wire recorder, the **telegraphone**. The word has three ideas in the roots that make up its name. *Tele* means "at a distance"; *graph* means "written" or "writing"; and *phone* means "sound" or "voice." From faraway distances and long ago times, people would be able to speak in a format that would become a permanent "text." Poulsen's telegraphone was the first machine to use magnetic recording to enhance the quality and scope of inventions like the phonograph and telephone.

Poulsen's machine recorded sound magnetically onto a steel wire (called "piano wire" by some). Like the phonograph, the steel wire reeled around the cylinder as sound was being captured. By studying the simpler versions of the phonograph and incorporating Smith's ideas, Poulsen approached magnetic technology with fresh ambition. As a telephone engineer, the primary ideal behind his mission was to record telephone messages—a task that the phonograph could not handle.

In order to record messages from a telephone, the receiving machine would need to be electromagnetic. Since the sound was coming from a distance (as in *tele*-phone), there needed to be something—a *graph*—to remember and transcribe what happened over the wires. This feat was far more complex than the phonograph as it would need to both cover great distances and improve upon the distorted quality of Edison's efforts.

The key to Poulsen's successful telegraphone was the idea of using an **alternating current (AC)**, an electric current that can periodically reverse direction.

Using AC was first hypothesized by Smith. Yet it was Poulsen's application that succeeded. The AC came

# Magnetic Field of a Bar Magnet

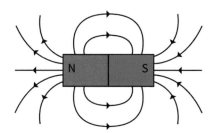

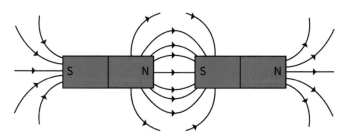

Attraction between opposite poles

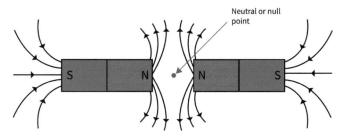

Repulsion between like poles

AC and electromagnets work together in the telegraphone.

from a telephone microphone signal. Poulsen sent an electromagnet along the steel wire. Electric signals mirrored the sound being recorded and then fed to the recording head, as suggested in Smith's diagram.

Poulsen's telegraphone wasn't yet electronic (though it was electric), but it did record sound that could be transmitted over telephone wires. The clarity of recordings was strong—much stronger than the phonograph. He presented his invention in 1900 at the World's Fair in Paris. At the exhibition, he recorded Emperor Franz Joseph of Austria. Today, the oldest magnetic sound recording still exists at the Danish Museum of Science and Technology. And with more advances in technology, you can even listen to it on YouTube.

Poulsen's telegraphone gave rise to a whole new relationship between people, technology, and media. People were excited, particularly because the process by which Poulsen recorded these voice transmissions seemed to be in direct opposition to what people believed magnets could do. Poulsen's use of AC as a means toward more electronic ends inspired scientists to expand their hypotheses and experiments in the field of electromagnetism. Eventually this more complicated understanding of magnets would pave the way for many more innovations in music, and later, in cinema. The telegraphone may not have done well as a commercial product, but its legacy has continued staying power in electronics today.

After the success of the telegraphone, Poulsen and his assistant continued experimenting with magnetism. This led Poulsen back toward transmission. He ended up creating the first continuous wave radio transmitter—the Poulsen arc transmitter—shortly after the World's Fair.

Camille and Henri Dreyfus developed cellulose acetate into a base for film.

His invention was well received and prevailed as common practice for radio transmission until other inventions entered the field two decades later.

# The INVENTION ITSELF

Fritz Pfleumer was an Austrian inventor living in Germany in the 1920s. Though economies were declining at that time, the demand for and sales of cigarettes boomed. In those days, the fancier cigarette brands used a gold leaf band to decorate the tips of the cigarette. To compete, cheaper brands used colored paper. The colored paper, though, left residue on smokers' lips. Consumers disliked this side effect, so manufacturers wanted a cheap alternative to the gold band that still matched its high-society aesthetic.

Pfleumer was a paper expert—special papers in particular. Instead of a band, he created a process that striped a gold line onto the cigarette. He used a powdered bronze to become the faux gold band for an everyman cigarette.

So how is it that we get from cigarettes to magnetic tape? Pfleumer figured that there must be a way to take his newly minted cigarette paper and replace the bronze with something magnetic. Poulsen had already presented a wire recording with his telegraphone. Using this hypothesis, Pfleumer began to take his cigarette paper and experiment with the world of the magnetic.

His desired effect was to record sound using magnetism. Pfleumer replaced the bronze dust of his cigarette papers with crushed iron. In 1928, Pfleumer received a German patent. He called his product "sounding paper." He even devised the first tape recorder to accompany his sounding paper during demonstrations. Though it didn't produce the best sound, it did the job well enough to garner excitement.

# The Mechanics of Recording on Magnetic Tape

With his patent in hand, Pfleumer began to seek help from larger manufacturers. He wanted his invention to become a commercial product, just like his cigarette paper.

AEG, a German electronics company, took on Pfleumer's project. Magnetics, as led by the inventions of Poulsen, seemed to be moving toward telecommunications. AEG thought this pursuit would complement the work they were doing in telecommunications, especially with the burgeoning use of radio as a way to get news out to the public. AEG's chairman, Privy Counselor Hermann Bücher, assembled a team of engineers to develop Pfleumer's magnetic tape.

Like the gramophone record, chemistry would need to play a role in the mass production of this kind of tape. Carbonyl iron was a common chemical used in the industry for high-frequency coils (used in telephones, for example), among other things. IG Farben (IG Farbenindustrie Aktiengesellschaft in German) was a gigantic chemical manufacturer in Germany that Bücher maintained working relations with. Together, the team of scientists worked to produce tape and a recorder.

To improve the product, the team used scientific methods of experimentation. In the laboratory, they coated sheets and strips of paper with carbonyl iron. To test the tape, they built an "endless-loop apparatus." The machine was able to reel 40 feet (12 meters) of tape from one magnetic head to another. The heads were shaped like chisels. Wound in coils, these cores worked well with steel wire, but not with paper. The paper tape often got stuck, or worse, tore. Paper was also difficult to work with because of its sensitivity to temperature. Pfleumer foresaw this as being a complication when he applied for the patent. To get the preferred effect, he recommended cellulose acetate as an alternative to paper.

# COMPUTERS and MAGNETIC TAPE

Alan Turing machines, or what we know today as computers, were being developed after World War II. Though they were decades away from becoming household items, the power of Turing's thinking machine was alluring to all. One of the problems with computer development was data storage and speed. Magnetic tape promised to address this issue, though it wouldn't be until the invention of vacuum tubes for televisions, computers, and other electronics in the late 1940s that this problem would begin to resolve itself more fully.

Cellulose acetate is a natural plastic. Its properties show that Pfleumer's hypothesis would lead to a desired result: cellulose acetate is resistant to water, nonpoisonous to human skin, highly machinable, and able to be coated in other chemicals.

By 1933, AEG was responsible for building a working tape recorder, while IG Farben's chemist, Friedrich Matthias, was tasked with developing the best magnetic tape to suit Pfleumer's vision. The whole year was dedicated to using the scientific method in experiments. The results were quite good as the signal-to-noise ratio improved from the paper version.

Meanwhile, AEG's machine for recording and testing was built as a mini film projector. The machine was built vertically. The double-flanged spoons "transported tape at 1 m/s [40 inches/second]." They began with five-minute reels. The chisel-shaped cores were replaced with ring-shaped tape heads, which lasted through the invention of **cassette tapes** and VHS tapes. Similar to Poulsen's telegraphone, AC was used to improve the sound recordings on magnetic tape.

# RECEPTION

The **AEG Magnetophon tape recorder** premiered in 1935 at the Berlin International Radio Exhibition. This first reel-to-reel tape recorder used the Pfleumer magnetic tape and was meant for everyday use. Because the Magnetophon was expensive and complicated, it was found mostly in recording studios and radio stations.

## Telecommunications Revolution

Pfleumer's magnetic tape and magnetic recording were revolutionary. Broadcast and recording industries would never be the same again. The tapes promised tremendous amounts of uninterrupted data.

Tape was inexpensive and ripe for mistake making. From the beginning, Pfleumer saw paper as being a weakness. It could rip easily. And even before the switch to cellulose acetate as the base for tape, he was rebranding this weakness as a positive: paper cost less to fix with tape or glue than the steel wire breaks of Poulsen's machine. By the time the cellulose acetate was the base, this idea of cutting the tape became another point of sale as **splicing** and multiple takes became new means of editing.

Where a gramophone record required one clean take, a tape could be rewound and recorded anew. A recorded performance could be edited. And as film, television, and radio boomed, tape editing was a common practice. An editor could physically cut the tape, rearrange the order, cut out frames, and create a reel that seemed to have been recorded in succession (still called "splicing" to this day).

As for broadcasting, magnetic tape revolutionized television and radio. At a time when everything was live, producers now had a way to prerecord their shows and broadcast them once they were edited. This allowed for multiple takes, time, and a perfected final product.

## Music Revolution

Music production began to change at the advance of magnetic tape in two key ways: audio fidelity and multiple takes. Artists could record a song multiple times on one roll of tape by either rewinding it or splicing together the portions that worked best. The sound quality and playback consistency made the magnetic tape superior to the gramophone record of the time. Performances also weren't bound to the thirty-minute time limit of a record.

Another reason magnetic tape gained traction in the music industry relates to America's Great Depression and the rise of commercial radios. In the 1920s, as radios were mass-produced for households, the record began to decline. Record companies started to forbid their artists from working directly with radio. This attempt didn't work, and record sales plummeted further, especially as the economy crashed. At this time, Bell was working to improve the fidelity of its records and introduced electric amplification and electronic recording.

Though magnetic tape wouldn't be a household means of playing music for some time, the rise of television and radio broadcast in music and news would make tape an industry standard.

# MAGNETIC TAPE in SOUND and IMAGING

At the end of World War II in the mid-1940s, the Allies investigated German radio and electronic activities. Two Magnetophon recorders and over fifty reels of IG Farben magnetic tape were recovered from a radio station outside of Frankfurt. (Seeing the value of the technology, the Nazis had attempted to keep it secret.) American audio engineer Jack Mullin studied the machines and tapes and decided to develop them for commercial use.

American singer, actor, and radio star Bing Crosby invested in magnetic tape immediately. At a minimum, he figured he could prerecord his radio shows. Crosby was the first artist to master commercial recordings on tape. An established American tape recording industry promptly followed.

Hollywood followed too, making Mullin's ambitions come true. Mullin's Magnetophone became the Magnetrack. He started a film recording business. Filmmakers took to magnetic tape for film and sound hastily. These new technologies allowed for swifter sound edits with better audio fidelity.

The reel-to-reel model of tape recording as begun by AEG's Magnetophon was a mainstay in tape-recording practices until the 1960s.

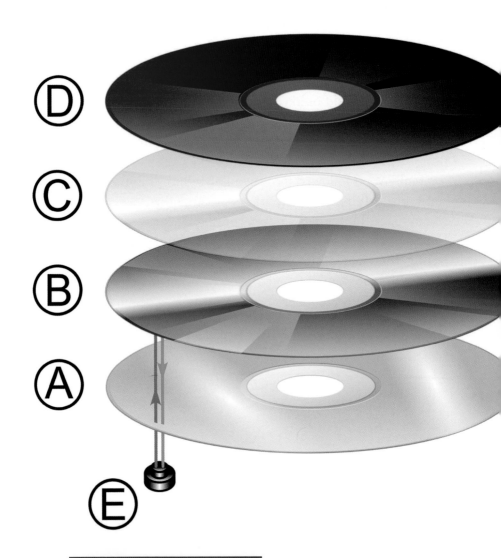

CDs are made up of multiple layers of materials, though the layers are hidden from the naked eye.

# CHAPTER 5
# MP3s

MP3 files revolutionized the way the public accesses, collects, shares, and listens to music. Unlike many other inventions in music, the MP3 was not generated from within the industry. Instead, its impact forced the industry to change to keep up. MP3s make good on the promise of the internet at large: free access to data, which in this case are song files. On the other side of the coin are new controversies in music: piracy, copyright law, artistic integrity, and corporate greed. These issues can be problematic for musicians and the art that they make.

## INVENTIONS That LED to the MP3

### Compact Disc (CD)

In Japan in 1982, Billy Joel's album *52nd Street* became the first commercially released **CD**. Philips and Sony worked together to make the audio disc. Like the phonograph, the arrival of the CD was an overnight sensation. Initially, CDs were pursued by manufacturers as a replacement for records. Ironically, as Sony and Philips effectively ended the use of the record, they received a technical Grammy for their work.

By the 1990s, CDs were the preferred form of data storage—and not just for music. At the time, a CD could hold more than early personal computers. Floppy discs became CD-ROMs. Cassettes became CDs. The Walkman personal music player became a Discman.

CDs brought huge advantages to users. Instead of having to fast forward and rewind to find a song on a cassette tape, this plastic, shiny disc featured tracks as separate, readable points. This feature also translated when film moved from VHS tapes to DVDs.

CD manufacturing followed the same scientific logic of a gramophone record. A single, spiral track of data is imprinted onto the plastic disc. We can't see or feel the spiral as it's made of microscopic bumps. Despite its thin size, a CD is made up of layers. Polycarbonate plastic is the base. That's where the spiral track goes. On top of that is a layer of aluminum (not unlike the tinfoil of Edison's old phonograph), which locks the little bumps of information into the plastic. A layer of acrylic is then sprayed on top of the aluminum to protect it. The label of the artist or disc brand is printed onto the acrylic.

The microscopic bumps on a CD are cut into the polycarbonate plastic with a laser. Along the spiral, there are gaps in the bumps to signal a new track. Despite this enigmatic façade, CDs were so cheap to make that they became rampant.

# CD Players

CD players were built to read the tiny, microscopic markings on the CD. Despite being a simple machine in its mechanics, a CD player must be highly intelligent and efficient to be able to read such small material. CD players have three main parts: a drive motor that spins the CD at the precise rate needed for playback, a lens and laser that work together to focus on and read the spiral of bumps, and

Inside of a CD player, there are many wires, magnets, lasers, and lenses that read and transmit the information on a CD.

a tracking mechanism at that moves the laser precisely in conjunction with the microscopic bumps.

Sony invented the Discman to rival and eventually replace the Walkman. From manufacturing costs to increased demand for CDs, these laser technologies took over the former power of the magnetic tape.

# The Rise of Software

Unlike making a cassette tape, making a custom CD was a matter of software. Whereas the hardware of a tape recorder was simple, making your own audio or data CD is more complex. Because of technological advancements and the rise of software, users with computers don't need to know anything about how a CD is made to make one themselves. The software takes the desired data and encodes it.

We see this today when using iTunes. If you wanted to have a playlist on a CD for a throwback boombox party, you simply ask your software to "export" the playlist and then wait. The user has no idea how the software or computer go about making a digital list a printed object. This endeavor was necessary in the 1990s and early 2000s before portable digital audio players—namely the iPod—were invented.

Software, personal computers, CDs, and other modern innovations mark a huge shift in technology from analog to digital. While in earlier machines, AC was once introduced as revolutionary, it was replaced handily with digitization of information. Instead of using electronic signals of varying frequency and amplitude, information is coded in numbers and symbols.

So what are the advantages of digital over analog? Looking back at the cause and effect of many inventions in audio technology, a common factor in the need for new inventions is the relationship between a product's cost and its quality. The greater the audio fidelity, for example, the

# DIGITAL AUDIO TAPE (DAT)

Sony introduced its **Digital Audio Tape** in 1987. It seemed a practical measure to take with the rise of the CD and the dwindling use of the cassette tape. This smaller cartridge still looked like and acted like a cassette for the most part. However, because the tape was digitized, it was able to compete with the CD. The tape was able to record and read IDs and numbers so that a user could search tracks separately. DATs never made it to the consumer market, though. It met fervent resistance from producers, composers, and other industry types. A DAT had the most superior sound quality to date and threatened an increase in piracy of audio information. If consumers could use a DAT to record a television show or radio song to near perfect duplication, piracy would be rampant.

Sony's DAT also posed larger threats within the industry. Using DATs could allow networks and record studios to steal information from each other. Though the Recording Industry Association of America was unsuccessful in their lobbying efforts, their threats against manufacturers worked, and DAT's reputation stayed quite small and away from the general public. The only place it survives now is in film and television recording.

more expensive the machine. When information is coded, it functions like a math equation: 1 + 1 = 2. You can type that in any font and the cause and effect are still the same. In digital software and hardware, the numbers will always be precise and translatable. You can listen to the same file on your headphones, iPad, laptop, and Wi-Fi speakers. The quality of the file will always be perfect and retained. The only things that might change are related hardware— like better speakers for less static, or surround sound for improved movie viewing. Likewise, in an age of Wi-Fi and internet dependence, companies who sell internet access to you have control over how strong or weak a signal may be.

# The INVENTION ITSELF

Initial MP3 efforts began in 1982 when German audio engineer Karlheinz Bradenburg started working on digital music compression. His doctoral work studied how people perceive music. It took until 1991 for industry standards (on formatting and such) to be solidified. MP3 went public in 1995. This free, swift, accessible file encoding process would snowball into the music industry and change it—for better or worse—into contemporary times.

## The Mechanics of MP3 Files

MP3 files as we know them were created by computer engineers because internet users are music lovers and had no specific way to encounter music on the internet. In order to bring music into the virtual world of cyberspace, file storage and transmission would need to be as small as possible without compromising audio fidelity. Without this desired effect, it would be difficult to help

MP3s and other digital files are now right at our fingertips with file sharing devices and apps like iTunes, Spotify, Pandora, SoundCloud, and more.

the public change the way they share, collect, distribute, and listen to music.

An MP3 uses the CD model at its core. Like CDs, MP3s take digital data and compress it. But how is it that an MP3 can make a file smaller without degrading the quality of a song? Algorithms help an MP3 read a digital file by scanning the sound information and choosing what to ignore. Multiple frequencies can be found at any given moment in a song. The compression algorithm assesses the frequencies and retains the loudest ones while ignoring the others. This process is called **perceptual noise shaping**. The key to understanding this technique is "perceptual." In transferring and compressing data, the MP3 accounts for truths about the human sound perception by ignoring sounds and pitches that can't be heard by the human ear. The algorithm maintains sounds the human ear hears well and ignores the softer frequencies when two things are played simultaneously since the human ear can hear only the louder ones anyway. Therefore, an MP3 file does not contain every element of sound from its digital source, but it achieves the desired effect of a very small file that is easy to download, distribute, share, and collect.

Because MP3s do not retain everything from their original source, their format is qualified as **lossy**. There are lossless compressions, but these techniques result in, of course, a larger file size. The spectrum of lossy format compressions relates primarily to **bit rate**. "Bit rate" refers to the number of bits encoded into a file. Cause and effect comes into play here too. When downloading and compressing a music file, many programs allow users to select a bit rate. The lower the bit rate, the more information the encoding logarithm will discard. The inverse is true, too: the higher the bit rate, the less information will be lost from the original to the MP3. This whole process is a mirror image to digital imaging. It's why art photographers' work still looks substantially better than our iPhones or point-and-shoot cameras—they are shooting and editing from much larger files than our Instagram accounts can handle.

# RECEPTION

## Instant Access

MP3 files changed the public's relationship to music instantly. MP3s and the internet have made it easy for anyone to find and access music. It became virtually free to distribute music, which has pros and cons for artists and record labels alike.

Further, MP3 files were one of the first modes of use people found with their computers outside of word processing. Pro Tools—a music editing software—was already in use by studios. By the time people were downloading MP3s, they were learning a lot about the enigmatic machine we call a personal computer.

In order to use an MP3, a layperson must figure out how to download a file. At the onset (though this is less popular now), people had to "rip" songs from their CDs to compress and download songs onto their computers or MP3 players. Likewise, people learned how to create a playlist and burn it onto a blank CD.

## Resistance of Audiophiles

Audiophiles are hi-fi (high fidelity) enthusiasts. While streaming and downloading are for the masses, vinyl is making a comeback among artists and audiophiles alike. Audiophiles dislike MP3s and claim that the sound files are inferior to CDs and records.

This resistance also comes from musicians and audio engineers. MP3 files have changed the production industry so much that many of them don't trust these "clean" sounding, basic files. Dynamics are a big part of what artists want to achieve in their work. Because studios are appealing to the masses, who primarily use MP3s in downloads and in streaming, the effect is a flattened editing process. Everything has begun to sound similar.

# LEGACIES

## File Sharing, Piracy, and Napster

The internet is an ongoing revolution that we are still figuring out today. One of the oldest case studies of the relationship between the internet, music, and copyright law is Napster. Napster was the first peer-to-peer (P2P) file-sharing service on the internet. Though other data could be shared, Napster was primarily used to share audio files.

Napster was developed by two teenagers: amateur web developers Shawn Fanning and Sean Parker. They launched their site on June 1, 1999. Less than a year later, over twenty million people were using Napster to share their music. The number of users grew from there.

For many, these figures were heroes of the new age. It used to be that if there was a new radio hit you loved, you'd have to go to the record store and buy the full CD just to get the one song you wanted to listen to on repeat. Now, not only was music free, but you could pick through an album song by song. Instead of owning fifteen Britney Spears songs you'd never listen to, you could now have only "... Baby One More Time."

But to many, Napster was evil. Many musicians hated it. Before Napster, it was hard enough to make it as an artist

The original file sharing platform—
Napster—generated controversy
across the world. What is sharing?
Stealing? Remix? Only time (and
changing laws) will tell!

because the middleman—the record label—takes home a far larger percentage from sales than the musicians. Now, people's lifework was being handed away for free to the masses. Record labels hated it the most, as there were no financial incentives for sharing music for free.

Napster's days were numbered. Shawn Fanning hadn't secured the rights to any of the music that was being shared. Just over a year after the launch of Napster, the Recording Industry Association of America (RIAA) brought a lawsuit against the file-sharing service in conjunction with some of music's biggest names. Napster shut down in July of 2001. Napster ended up paying millions of dollars to artists and copyright holders.

The issues that Napster evoked are still controversial today. As technology continues to change our access to things in the world, the extent to which copyright can protect people's intellectual and artistic information is increasingly up for grabs. On the other hand, Napster had its fair share of supporters from musicians who were excited to see their songs shared around the world. Napster unearthed other complicated questions about the industry and about capitalism at large. Who should have the rights to these songs? Who should get paid? Who should do the paying? Who should have control? It is those questions that continue to be answered and asked as technology holds an increasing power over our day-to-day lives.

# The Music Industry's New Normal

MP3s and the internet upon which they exist forced the world of music to change utterly. From producing to distribution to instruments, we are in a digital time.

For the most part, the idea of an album fell out of fashion in the late nineties. As people could download singles and ignore the songs that didn't make it to the radio's "top forty," the meaning behind a full album became worthless. For pop artists seeking quick fame, this may have been fine, but for artists of older eras, audiophiles, and the like, this change in the art itself causes melancholy and nostalgia for a different time when music itself was at the forefront rather than the industry and public recognition.

Napster utterly disrupted the industry model. After decades of perfect crafting, middlemen—from managers, to studio heads, to producers, to labels—saw the potential for their cuts (which are higher than the artists') per record sold to evaporate entirely. Napster showed the world that many of them would no longer be relevant. The combination of this internet truth with the rise of the MP3 had them scrambling to beat hackers to remodeling their industry.

Many clubs have replaced live music stages with DJ booths and elaborate light shows, a sign of changing times in music.

# CHAPTER 6
# The Future of Music

L ike any other time of great change, the digital world has presented musicians and industry leaders with exciting new horizons and plenty of complications and trying challenges along the way. A young child's introduction to music is more likely to be through GarageBand on their laptop than an instrument (a piano costs a whole lot more than a laptop …). Thanks to the influence of computers, new genres have entered the scene under the larger categories of dance and electronic, including EDM, dubstep, techno, trance, two-step, and electronica. While we still have pop sensations and bands, DJs have become their equals.

Digital technologies have also caused a lot of changes to who is "discovered" and how. Stages have been replaced with online or on-camera platforms. Stars are found through reality TV shows and YouTube. Rapid change seems to be the only constant in music these days.

## NEW TOOLS and NEW SOUNDS

Since the start of the millennium, sound engineers and DJs have been at the forefront of commercial sound. To help them, many new tools have hit the market, allowing DJs and producers to stay on the cutting edge.

## Pro Tools

The first version of Pro Tools was released in the mid-1980s, but the software wouldn't be ready for public consumption until 1991. Pro Tools was the first digital audio workstation. It functioned in conjunction with Microsoft software and eventually would be part of Avid editing (the main editing software for filmmakers until Final Cut Pro hit the market). Pro Tools is used for mixing multiple tracks. For example, if a lead vocalist is singing while playing guitar and has a bass player and drummer backing her up, a sound mixer will allow an editor to adjust the levels of each of those four instruments in conjunction with the physics of the human ear. This was so valuable that it cost about $6,000 when it was released. Nowadays, Apple computers come with GarageBand for free. Of course, different programs have different advantages and specialties.

## Auto-Tune

As the music of the late nineties and early aughts became more futuristic and electronic, music producers wanted human voices to match the digital reign. From Cher's "Believe" to every song by T-Pain, this more robotic, mechanical sound of the human voice has been crucial to our contemporary understanding of pop music. With the digital comes perfection. Auto-Tune can make every sung word sound perfectly produced. To this day, Auto-Tune sparks controversy. Many artists feel that it's inauthentic, ushering in a new meaning to "audio fidelity." Others embrace Auto-Tune as an instrument unto itself, one that, just like a guitar or a saxophone, has its own unique sound quality, mood, and function.

# CARSON DALY, MTV VJ

Carson Daly has championed the careers of many contemporary pop sensations throughout his time on *TRL* and *The Voice*.

Our most famous contemporary VJ, perhaps, is Carson Daly. Host of MTV's *Total Request Live* (also known as *TRL*) for five years, Daly was a staple item in the afternoons of young people all over America. Similar to the Top 40 format begun by DJs, *TRL* introduced the top-ten music videos of the day. In between videos, Daly would interview celebrities and introduce the songs to a live crowd in Times Square.

Eventually, music television lost popularity and was replaced by a new wave of reality TV. Daly has since been able to maintain a consistent career in television hosting and producing. In fact, he's currently the VJ of *The Voice*. Music and reality television have blended together. Instead of introducing videos, Daly now introduces performances by young singers, covering famous songs in hopes of catching a big break.

# The ROLE of the DJ (and VJ)

From the phonograph and gramophone, to amplifiers, microphones, magnetic tape, and CDs, the band was attuned to the promises and losses that twentieth-century inventions in media and arts presented to the public. The effect of these causes? Video killed the radio star. Transistor radios and the Walkman were already on the way out with the advance to prerecorded television. Bands could now lipsync to maintain audio fidelity. A music video could present the song as well as a narrative simultaneously. Listening was replaced by viewing. Materialism would rise as people could see the artist—their instruments, what they wore, how attractive they were. And thus, the "me" generation came into being. In the past, the band was replaced by the DJ. Now the DJ was being replaced by the VJ—the video jockey—a cast member to introduce music videos.

While music television was on the rise, DJs of the 1980s became more of an underground sensation where music clubs would allow. Some clubs converted their interior to include projections of music videos (and later, light shows) as a replacement for the disco ball. Africa Bambaataa was the first DJ to use a synthesizer in a song. DJs were using new technologies to change sound altogether. Tracks could be filled with electronic sounds played at a tempo and be considered music. Everything sounded like electricity.

Chicago's Warehouse Club was a famous reclaimed space in which DJs spun house music—disco tracks with electro beats. New York took notes from Chicago's house music and spun them to become New York garage. Detroit DJs took the best of Chicago, New York, and Europe and created techno music.

Another landmark event occurred in 1985: Run DMC and Aerosmith collaborated on "Walk This Way." It was the first song featuring hip-hop to make *Billboard's* top-ten hits list. And it was the first time a DJ was considered part of a band.

It isn't until the 1990s that the superstar DJ became a cultural figure. While DJ music was once representative of the underground, technological advancement would turn the audio engineer into a star.

During the 1990s, the rave scene changed the image of the DJ. With values of material and brand names changing the public consciousness in the 1980s, the DJs of the 1990s became their own brand. They had to brand their sound, their name, their style. Music was not only about music and dancing, but rather an atmosphere designed by a DJ.

Because sound had changed so much, the effect was a different kind of music. Every element was electric and virtually nothing was vocal or made by a traditional instrument. Basslines, electro beats, and synth sounds could be digitally manipulated and recorded in conjunction with scratch sounds and other inventive modes of sound making.

Further, DJs of the 1990s began to gain advantages from the internet. The first internet radio stations came into being, meaning people from all over the world could access the same radio show, unlike the physics of old radio stations and wires.

MP3s changed the life of DJs utterly. The promise of what could be controlled and manipulated digitally was intoxicating, not to mention not having to lug a trunk's worth of CDs or vinyl around. Napster also instigated a new system for DJs. DJs could apply for a license to use tracks stored on a hard drive at live shows.

DJ culture is no longer underground but rather mainstream. Though few of us can name DJs of the past, we can all name DJs of our contemporary time. From Calvin Harris, Tiesto, and Deadmau5, to Skrillex, Above&Beyond, and hundreds of others, much of what we hear today is touched by a DJ.

EDM (electronic dance music) is one of our fastest-growing commercial music markets. One of the large controversies these days, though, is the authenticity of the DJ's work. Where older DJs had to beatmatch, scratch, and lay tracks on the fly, contemporary DJs can play a sold-out show by pressing play on a prerecorded mix. Further, like many things commercial, the DJ superstar scene is dominated by men. There are plenty of women who are DJs, yet they have not been afforded the same consideration as their male counterparts. The DJ life is at a tipping point now that it's become so popular. Hopefully, like many moments of change, the women who are making awesome music in an underground scene will come to the forefront and change music once again.

## Remix Culture

Music and music inventions of our era have helped remix culture spread. Remix culture was coined by Lawrence Lessig in his 2008 book *Remix*, which addresses various cultural phenomena that all come back to the idea of remix. Remix cultures engender derivative works and hybridization as a form of creativity.

To Lessig, this mode of sharing of information is beneficial to all. He founded the Creative Commons to that end. Creative Commons still exists and releases licenses to the public so various source materials can be used for remixing—that goes from songs, to books, to brand names, and the like. His model owes much to the earlier movement developed by software writers, the free and open-source software movement, which allows appropriation of various parts of software for other designers than the original writer.

Though many kinds of cultural works can be generated through this culture, music is at the forefront in exploring the meaning. After all, DJs are responsible for slightly altering songs—from tempo changes, to mash-ups, to song blending and beyond.

## Remix or Stealing?

Though Lessig has a democratic view of remix culture, it has caused many controversies about intellectual and artistic property. Intellectuals, writers, and artists have historically been mistreated by capitalism. Though the public loves artists, the artist is not protected by the industries that make money off of her. By adding remix to the already complex legal system around copyright laws, company ethics (and the lack thereof) and industry standards cause a lot of controversy on all sides.

With few artists in control of the consumption of their work, it's been very difficult to police breaks in copyright law. Likewise, copyright laws are becoming more and more flexible with the onset of the internet and its free access to data. Some artists remix in the form of sample. A popular example of this is the origin of the song "Good Feeling." A sample from singer Etta James's song "Something's Got a Hold on Me" was used by Avicii in the track "Levels." That remix was then sampled and used by Flo Rida in his song "Good Feeling." The repeated clip "oh, oh, sometimes / I get a good feeling, yeah, / I get a feeling that I never, never, never, never had before, oh yeah, / I get a good feeling …" has been remixed and remade so many times it's hard to remember the point of origin at all, let alone hear it.

# BEYONCÉ and the ARTIST'S STRUGGLE

While many artists are at the mercy of the industry, some of our most famous artists are great models of excellence on their own terms. For her two most recent albums, Beyoncé Knowles has shown the public the potential power of the artist to fight all kinds of cultural wrongs.

Her self-titled album of 2013, *Beyoncé*, was memorable for many reasons, foremost that it dropped on Friday the 13th of December, 2013, with no warning. There had been no leaked singles, no promotion, no announcements. Just a sudden album release with a full video album to accompany it. The album featured many other artists, homages to different music cultures, samples, and the like.

Her album *Lemonade* and its accompanying "visual album" have also been viral successes. The issues of *Lemonade* cut even deeper than her past albums. The space is filled with black women exclusively. The content of the songs deals with all kinds of hardships that black women and women at large face. And further, the video album even more directly appropriates images and words from other artists. Some of the interludes are poems by Somali-British poet Warsan Shire. Beyoncé wears a yellow Roberto Cavalli dress to imitate and honor African goddess Oshun, the Yoruba deity of love.

Works like *Lemonade* and Claudia Rankine's book *Citizen* (see page 92) radically offer the world new ways of thinking. One cannot leave the spaces created by these works without rethinking history and culture. Rankine and Knowles have supported the art of others and brought those works into the popular consciousness. This kind of support shows remix as activism and engagement in social justice.

Beyoncé Knowles onstage in Pasadena, California, performing a concert during the Formation World Tour.

# STREAMING

Napster marked a huge shift toward remix culture. Computer engineers were already paving the way with shared data (between each other and the public), while corporations were holding on the promises of 1980s capitalism. Newspapers and magazines that resisted digitization began to fail and fold. Radio shows that resisted internet hosting were destined to fail. Banks without digital banking wouldn't make it to the crash of 2008, let alone through it. The tide had changed already.

As a result of increased access, other tech innovators took Napster's ideals and created a more legal means of giving the public what they wanted. We now primarily stream music. Whether we listen for free on SoundCloud or YouTube, or pay for memberships to Amazon Prime or Spotify, or suffer through ads on the free version of Pandora, the experience of home listening has been changed completely from the days of the phonograph.

# REMIXING: BEYOND MUSIC

Remix is being reclaimed by many artists in many genres. Claudia Rankine's book *Citizen* repurposes famous images, her own poetry, and text and still shots from installations into one space. At her readings, a projector is used while she reads. She often shows slides of the images of her books. Her video installations that braid news footage, her own words, and music together are also presented. The premise of this work is more in line with Lessig's altruistic vision of remix culture: a curated cultural experience resulting in a new idea.

Claudia Rankine's *Citizen* is the first book to be nominated in both the poetry and criticism categories for the National Book Critics Circle Award.

# MUSIC, EVOLVING
## with US

Though many technologies have advanced the music industry, musical instruments, music production, music collecting, music distribution, and music sharing, one thing has remained unchanged: music as evolution. From Darwin until now, music is at the center of survival.

In contemporary times, we may think of this as political survival first. Many music superstars consider their work a platform for larger cultural change. The rock 'n' roll messages of political frustration and a desire for peace during the counterculture movement of the 1960s and 70s showed a collective of musicians after a larger message. In America right now, there are many musicians fighting the good fight.

Music has always been the voice behind revolution. Politics are only adequate to make change after the tides of consciousness have shifted. So by the time, for example, that American schools were desegregated, there had already been many songs in the public vernacular used for power, bonding, coping, and inspiration.

And beneath that truth is the evolution of our feelings. As individuals and communities experience life, music is often the backdrop. Our habits of mind and heart have scores that illuminate the mood and meaning of any given occasion. No matter how far technology has gone, the central idea of ritual has stayed intact. Our rituals may involve new instruments of expression, but the desire for ritual continues to foreground our ability to survive or not.

In scholarship, once a language is lost, it marks the end of a given civilization or society. For example, Sephardic Jews spoke a language called Ladino, which blended Hebrew and Spanish together. After the Spanish Inquisition and the Holocaust, the survival of Sephardim has dwindled substantially. While Yiddish of the Ashkenazi Jews has seen a slight revival, there aren't enough Sephardim to remember and revive Ladino. All that remains intact are songs. They're the last emblem of this ghost language and the people who used to speak it.

Music and its preservation, then, stand for our survival. From the sounds of speaking to song, music traces a path to the beginning of time. The physical and digital artifacts it leaves behind are fossils of the soul.

# GLOSSARY

**AEG Magnetophon tape recorder** The first tape recorder made by Fritz Pfleumer and AEG; the first reel-to-reel tape recorder made for everyday use, later modified for better sound quality.

**alternating current (AC)** An electric current that constantly reverses its direction.

**analog** Data represented by continuously moving parts (as in AC).

**bit rate** The number of bits or 1s that a digital network can transmit per second.

**cassette tape** A plastic cartridge containing a pair of spools and a length of magnetic tape, upon which to record or playback audio or video content; this takes the form of a compact cassette tape for audio and VHS tape for video.

**CD** A compact disc; a plastic disc able to store music or other digital files on it.

**chord** An effect produced when sounding multiple notes (usually three) simultaneously, making up the basis of harmony.

**cuneiform** Wedge-shaped characters that make up the protolanguage of non-Semitic Mesopotamian civilizations, especially Sumer.

**diaphragm** A taut, flexible sheet of material in acoustic systems, meant to mimic the dome-shaped partition of the same name between the thorax and abdomen; in breathing and in sound machines, contraction increases volume (of air).

**diatonic scale** Dating back to Pythagoras's development of the monochord, this set of seven notes—A to G—make up the common sounds of Western music to this day.

**Digital Audio Tape (DAT)** A magnetic tape that can store and play back digital data.

**fidelity** Audio fidelity refers to how closely a recording replicates its source.

**graphophone** An improved phonograph by Alexander Graham Bell and Volta Laboratories, which recorded sound into wax in an up-and-down fashion, enhanced from the original stylus-on-tinfoil printings of Edison's phonograph.

**harmony** A combination of chords and chord progressions resulting in a pleasing effect. In Pythagoras's initial definition of harmony, a pleasing whole was to be the result (making a relationship between Earth and the cosmos, unlike the music-specific definition we use today).

**headphones** Known as "cans" at the onset, Nathaniel Baldwin's headphones were originally made of copper wiring and an operator's headband. They were uninteresting to manufacturers, but the Navy ended up buying copious amounts of them in anticipation of war. He made them by hand in his kitchen.

**interval** The difference between musical notes.

**lossy** A qualifier to data compression that discards unneeded information from the original source material.

**magnetic tape** Plastic tape that's coated in chemicals in order to record sound, images, or computer data.

**metronome** A device used by musicians to mark time; a ticker that can be set at different rates for the purpose of regulating musical time.

**microphone** An instrument invented by David Edward Hughes (though Edison scored the first patent) that converts sound waves into electric energy, which is then amplified, transmitted, or recorded.

**monochord** From the Greek meaning "one string," an ancient instrument used to play and study the relationship between musical pitches.

**motherese** Speech directed at babies, or "baby talk."

**MP3** A way to compress and transmit sound through small files.

**note** A musical sound that has a definite pitch.

**octave** An interval between notes in which the higher note has twice the frequency of the lower note. In a scale, the upper note closes one octave and serves to begin another.

**paleophone** Invented by the French poet Charles Cros, this almost-phonograph's name translates to "voice of the past."

**perceptual noise shaping** A technique used to compress digital song files into MP3 format in which some parts of a digital file are abandoned without the human ear recognizing the omission(s).

**phonautogram** A tracing of a recording in the form of undulating lines on lampblack-coated parchment.

**phonautograph** A machine used to record and reproduce sound.

**pitch** The frequency of a given musical note; the higher the note, the higher the pitch, and vice versa.

**songline** An Australian Aboriginal practice and belief in which a song is used to navigate a path through a landscape in preliterate/premapping times; also seen in other cultures and languages.

**splicing** In film and sound editing, connecting or reweaving footage together.

**stylus** A hard point following a groove in a record to transmit the recorded sound.

**telegraphone** An electromagnetic phonograph invented by Valdemar Poulsen.

**tuning fork** Musicians use this two-pronged steel device to determine pitch.

# BIBLIOGRAPHY

Ashton, Anthony. *Harmonograph: A Visual Guide to the Mathematics of Music*. New York: Walker & Company, 2003.

Brain, Marshall. "How CDs Work." How Stuff Works: Tech, April 1, 2000. Accessed April 12, 2016. http://electronics.howstuffworks.com/cd1.htm.

————. "How MP3 Files Work." How Stuff Works: Tech. April 1, 2000. Accessed April 16, 2016. http://computer.howstuffworks.com/mp3.htm.

Cunningham, Erin. "Why Beyoncé Wore That Lemonade Dress." *Refinery 29*, April 27, 2016. Accessed April 27, 2016. http://www.refinery29.com/2016/04/109393/beyonce-lemonade-yellow-dress-oshun-roberto-cavalli.

Daniel, Eric D., C. Denis Mee, and Mark H. Clark, eds. *Magnetic Recording: The First 100 Years*. New York: IEEE Press, 1999.

Darwin, Charles. *The Descent of Man, and Selection in Relation to Sex*. Princeton, NJ: Princeton University Press, 1981.

"Evolution of DJ Technology." Dawsons, June 3, 2013. Accessed April 16, 2016. http://www.dawsons.co.uk/blog/evolution-of-dj-technology.

Herzog, Kenny. "24 Inventions That Changed Music." *Rolling Stone*, March 17, 2014. Accessed April 5, 2016. http://www.rollingstone.com/music/pictures/24-inventions-that-changed-music-20140317.

"Inventing the Wire Recorder." The History of Sound Recording. Accessed April 12, 2016. http://www.recording-history.org/HTML/wire2.php.

Jones, Josh. "Listen to the Oldest Song in the World: A Sumerian Hymn Written 3,400 Years Ago." Open Culture, July 8, 2014. Accessed April 27, 2016. http://www.openculture.com/2014/07/the-oldest-song-in-the-world.html.

Kilmer, Anne Draffkorn. "The Musical Instruments from Ur and Ancient Mesopotamian Music." *Expedition*, July 1998. Accessed April 27, 2016. http://www.penn.museum/sites/expedition/the-musical-instruments-from-ur-and-ancient-mesopotamian-music.

Klein, Christopher. "10 Things You May Not Know About Charles Darwin." History.com, February 12, 2014. Accessed April 2, 2016. http://www.history.com/news/10-things-you-may-not-know-about-charles-darwin.

Kusch, K. "Songlines: How Indigenous Australians Use Music to Mark Geography." The Basement Geographer, October 21, 2010. Accessed April 8, 2016. http://basementgeographer.com/songlines-how-indigenous-australians-use-music-to-mark-geography.

Locker, Melissa. "Beat Boys: The Rise of the Superstar DJ." *Time*, June 26, 2012. Accessed April 20, 2016. http:// entertainment.time.com/2012/06/26/beat-boys-the-rise-of-the-superstar-dj.

"Magnetic Tape Recording." Word Systems, Inc. Accessed April 8, 2016.http://www.wsystems.com/news/magnetic-tapes-recording.html.

"Modern Sound on Magnetic Tape." Modesto Radio Museum. Accessed April 8, 2016. http://www.modestoradiomuseum.org/magnetic%20tape.html.

"Music as Meaningful Vibrations." Ardue Hollistic Education. Accessed April 5, 2016. http://www.ardue.org.uk/university/intro/sound.html.

Newville, Leslie J. *Development of the Phonograph at Alexander Graham Bell's Volta Laboratory*. e-book. September 27, 2009.

Nicolaides, Demetris. *In the Light of Science: Our Ancient Quest for Knowledge and the Measure of Modern Physics*. Amherst, NY: Prometheus Books, 2014.

Owen, James. "Bone Flute Is Oldest Instrument, Study Says." NationalGeographic.com, June 24, 2009. Accessed April 5, 2016. http://news.nationalgeographic.com/news/2009/06/090624-bone-flute-oldest-instrument.html.

Smith, Oberlin. "Some Possible Forms of Phonograph." *Electrical World*. September 8, 1888.

Suskind, Alex. "15 Years After Napster: How the Music Service Changed the Industry." *Daily Beast*, June 6, 2014. Accessed April 16, 2016. http://www. thedailybeast.com/articles/2014/06/06/15-years-after-napster-how-the-music-service-changed-the-industry. html.

"Technology and the Recorded Music Industry." Music in Australia: Knowledge Base. Accessed April 17, 2016. http://www.musicinaustralia.org.au/index. php?title=Technology_and_the_Recorded_Music_ Industry.

Wellesz, Egon, ed. *The New Oxford History of Music I: Ancient and Oriental Music*. Oxford, UK: Oxford University Press, 1969.

# FURTHER INFORMATION

## Books

Hall, Manly P. *The Secret Teachings of All Ages.* Radford, VA: Wilder Publications, 2009.

Lessig, Lawrence. *Remix: Making Art and Commerce Thrive in a Hybrid Economy.* New York: Penguin Press, 2008.

Millard, Andre. *America on Record: A History of Recorded Sound.* New York: Cambridge University Press, 2005.

Stross, Randall. *The Wizard of Menlo Park: How Thomas Alva Edison Invented the Modern World.* New York: Three Rivers Press, 2007.

## Websites

**Computer History Museum**
http://www.computerhistory.org
The Computer History Museum preserves and presents artifacts and stories from the digital age. Within this history, machines like the telegraphone, phonograph, computers, and digital forms are represented.

**Incredibox**
http://www.incredibox.com
Incredibox is a free musical app in which you can quickly and easily create a mix by running a band of beatboxers.

### The Thomas Edison Center at Menlo Park
http://www.menloparkmuseum.org
Thomas Edison's laboratory and office—Menlo Park—have been reclaimed as a museum in his memory. The museum and its online archives preserve the history of the young, unknown man and his rise to fame through innovation.

# Films

### Downloaded
http://www.downloadedthemovie.com
*Downloaded* is a documentary film about digital media sharing. It uses the controversial company Napster as its centerpiece to explore the pros and cons of the digital revolution we are still experiencing today.

### Everything is a Remix
http://www.everythingisaremix.info/watch-the-series
This film explores different viewpoints and attitudes on intellectual property. Originally a four-part series, the film can now be viewed as one longer piece. Producer Kirby Ferguson can also be seen discussing the film in a TED Talk.

### 1900 Emperor Franz Joseph Oldest Magnetic Recording on Poulsen Telegraphone.
http://www.youtube.com/watch?v=pzrB_pwi2TM
The oldest magnetic recording, of Austrian emperor Franz Joseph, taped by telegraphone inventor Valdemar Poulsen at the 1900 World's Fair in Paris.

# Institutions/Companies

**MMMMaven Project**

http://www.mmmmaven.com

MMMMaven Project is a DJ school in Cambridge, Massachusetts, which teaches courses about digital music making. From the early onset of electronic music, to contemporary DJ equipment, MMMMaven helps students build valuable music production skills.

**Silk Road Project**

http://www.silkroadproject.org

Cellist Yo-Yo Ma founded the nonprofit foundation Silkroad in 1998. The Silk Road Ensemble was formed shortly thereafter as a way of bringing together innovative performers and composers representing traditions from around the world. Silkroad is the nexus of arts, education, and business.

# INDEX

# ABOUT the AUTHOR

**LISA HITON** is a filmmaker and poet from Deerfield, Illinois. She went to film school at Boston University where she first learned about sound design, magnetic tape, and editing. She teaches film, poetry, literature, and education at universities on the East Coast.